Adobe Photoshop CC Keyboard Shortcuts for Windows and Macintosh OS

By

U. C-Abel Books.

Published by U. C-Abel Books

Table of Contents

Acknowledgement.

All thanks to God Almighty for enabling us to bring this work to this point. He is a wonder indeed.

We want to specially appreciate the great company, Adobe Systems for their hard work and style of reasoning in providing the public with helpful programs and resources, and for helping us with some of the tips and keyboard shortcuts included in this book.

Dedication

The dedication of this title goes to users of Adobe Photoshop all over the world.

How We Began.

We enjoy using shortcuts because they set us on a high plane that astonishes people around us when we work with them. As wonderful shortcuts users, the worst eyesore we witness in computer operation is to see somebody sluggishly struggling to execute a task through mouse usage when in actual sense shortcuts will help to save that person time. Most people have asked us to help them with a list of keyboard shortcuts that can make them work as smartly as we do and that drove us into research to broaden our knowledge and truly help them as they demanded, that is the reason for the existence of this book. It is a great tool for lovers of shortcuts, and those who want to join the group.

Most times the things we love don't come by easily. It is our love for keyboard shortcuts that made us to bear long sleepless nights like owls just to make sure we get the best out of it, and it is the best we got that we are sharing with you in this book. You cannot be the same at computing after reading this book. The time you entrusted to our care is an expensive possession and we promise not to mess it up.

Thank you.

What to Know Before You Begin.

General Notes.

1. Most of the keyboard shortcuts you will see in this book refer to the U.S. keyboard layout. Keys for other layouts might not correspond exactly to the keys on a U.S. keyboard. Keyboard shortcuts for laptop computers might also differ.

2. It is important to note that when using shortcuts to perform any command, you should make sure the target area is active, if not, you may get a wrong result. Example, if you want to highlight all texts you must make sure the text field is active and if an object, make sure the object area is active. The active area is always known by the location where the cursor of your computer blinks.

3. On a Mac keyboard, the Command key is denoted with the ⌘ symbol.

4. If a function key doesn't work on your Mac as you expect it to, press the Fn key in addition to the function key. If you don't want to press the Fn key every time, you can change your Apple system preferences.

5. The plus (+) sign that comes in the middle of keyboard shortcuts simply means the keys are

meant to be combined or held down together not to be added as one of the shortcut keys. In a case where plus sign is needed; it will be duplicated (++).

6. Many keyboards assign special functions to function keys, by default. To use the function key for other purposes, you have to press Fn+the function key.

7. For keyboard shortcuts in which you press one key immediately followed by another key, the keys are separated by a comma (,).

8. For chapters that have more than one topic, search for "A fresh topic" to see the beginning of a topic, and "End of Topic" to see the end of a topic.

9. It is also important to note that the keyboard shortcuts, tips, and techniques listed in this book are for users of Adobe Photoshop CC.

10. To get more information on this title visit ucabelbooks.wordpress.com and search the site using keywords related to it.

11. Our chief website is under construction.

Some Short Forms You Will Find in This Book and Their Full Meaning.

Here are short forms used in this Adobe Photoshop CC Keyboard Shortcuts for Windows and Macintosh OS book and their full meaning.

1. Win - Windows logo key
2. Tab - Tabulate Key
3. Shft - Shift Key
4. Prt sc - Print Screen
5. Num Lock - Number Lock Key
6. F - Function Key
7. Esc - Escape Key
8. Ctrl - Control Key
9. Caps Lock - Caps Lock Key
10. Alt - Alternate Key

CHAPTER 1.

Fundamental Knowledge of Keyboard Shortcuts.

Without the existence of the keyboard, there wouldn't have been anything like keyboard shortcuts so in this chapter we will learn a little about the computer keyboard before moving to keyboard shortcuts.

1. Definition of Computer Keyboard.

This is an input device that is used to send data to computer memory.

Sketch of a Keyboard

1.1 Types of Keyboard.

   i. Standard (Basic) Keyboard.

  ii. Enhanced (Extended) Keyboard.

   i. **Standard Keyboard:** This is a keyboard designed during the 1800s for mechanical typewriters with just 10 function keys (F keys) placed at the left side of it.

  ii. **Enhanced Keyboard:** This is the current 101 to 102-key keyboard that is included in almost all the personal computers (PCs) of nowadays, which has 12 function keys, usually at the top side of it.

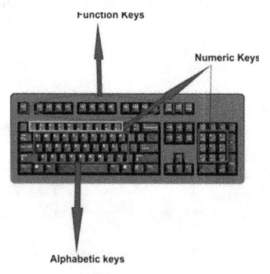

Function Keys

Numeric Keys

Alphabetic keys

1.2 Segments of the keyboard

- Numeric keys.
- Alphabetic keys.
- Punctuation keys.
- Windows Logo key.
- Function keys.
- Special keys.

Numeric Keys: Numeric keys are keys with numbers from **0 - 9**.

Alphabetic Keys: These are keys that have alphabets on them, ranging from **A** to **Z**.

Punctuation Keys: These are keys of the keyboard used for punctuation, examples include comma, full stop, colon, question marks, hyphen, etc.

Windows Logo Key: A key on Microsoft Computer keyboard with its logo displayed on it. Search for this 🪟 on your keyboard.

Apple Key: This also known as Command key is a modifier key that you can find on an Apple keyboard. It usually has the image of an apple or command logo on it. Search for this on your Apple keyboard ⌘

Function Keys: These are keys that have **F** on them which are usually combined with other keys. They are F1 - F12, and are also in the class called *Special Keys*.

Special Keys: These are keys that perform special functions. They include: Tab, Ctrl, Caps lock, Insert, Prt sc, alt gr, Shift, Home, Num lock, Esc, and many others. Special keys differ according to the type of computer involved. In some keyboard layout, especially laptops, the keys that turn the speaker on/off, the one that increases/decreases volume, the key that turns the computer Wifi on/off are also special keys.

Other Special Keys Worthy of Note.

Enter Key: This is located at the right-hand corner of most keyboards. It is used to send messages to the computer to execute commands, in most cases it is used to mean "Ok" or "Go".

Escape Key (ESC): This is the first key on the upper left of most keyboards. It is used to cancel routines, close menus and select options such as **Save** according to circumstances.

Control Key (CTRL): It is located on the bottom row of the left and right hand side of the keyboard. They also work with the function keys to execute commands using Keyboard shortcuts (key combinations).

Alternate Key (ALT): It is located on the bottom row also of some keyboard, very close to the CTRL key on both side of the keyboard. It enables many editing functions to be accomplished by using some keystroke combinations on the keyboard.

Shift Key: This adds to the roles of function keys. In addition, it enables the use of alternative function of a particular button (key), especially, those with more than one function on a key. E.g. use of capital letters, symbols, and numbers.

1.3. Selecting/Highlighting With Keyboard.

This is a highlighting method or style where data is selected using the computer keyboard instead of a computer mouse.

To do this:

- Move your cursor to the text or object you want to highlight, make sure that area is active,
- Hold down the shift key with one finger,
- Then use another finger to move the arrow key that points to the direction you want to highlight.

1.4 The Operating Modes Of The Keyboard.

Just like the computer mouse, keyboard has two operating modes. The two modes are Text Entering Mode and Command Mode.

a. **Text Entering Mode:** this mode gives the operator/user the opportunity to type text.
b. **Command Mode:** this is used to command the operating system/software/application to execute commands in certain ways.

2. Ways To Improve In Your Typing Skill.

1. Put Your Eyes Off The Keyboard.

This is the aspect of keyboard usage that many don't find funny because they always ask. "How can I put my eyes off the keyboard when I am running away from the occurrence of errors on my file?" My aim is to be fast, is this not going to slow me down?

Of course, there will be errors and at the same time your speed will slow down but the motive behind the introduction to this method is to make you faster than you are. Looking at your keyboard while you type can make you get a sore neck, it is better you learn to touch type because the more you type with your eyes fixed on the screen instead of the keyboard, the faster you become.

An alternative to keeping your eyes off your keyboard is to use the *"Das Keyboard Ultimate"*.

2. Errors Challenge You

It is better to fail than to not try at all. Not trying at all is an attribute of the weak and lazybones. When you make mistakes, try again because errors are opportunities for improvement.

3. Good Posture (Position Yourself Well).

Do not adopt an awkward position while typing. You should get everything on your desk organized or arranged before sitting to type. Your posture while typing contributes to your speed and productivity.

4. Practice

Here is the conclusion of everything said above. You have to practice your shortcuts constantly. The practice alone is a way of improvement. "Practice brings improvement". Practice always.

2.1 Software That Will Help You Improve Your Typing Skill.

There are several Software programs for typing that both kids and adults can use for their typing skill. Here is a list of software that can help you improve in your typing: Mavis Beacon, Typing Instructor, Mucky Typing Adventure, Rapid Tying Tutor, Letter Chase Tying Tutor, Alice Touch Typing Tutor and many more. Personally, I love Mavis Beacon.

To learn typing using MAVIS BEACON, install Mavis Beacon software to your computer, start with keyboard lesson, then move to games. Games like **Penguin Crossing, Creature Lab**, or **Space Junk** will help you become a professional in typing. Typing and keyboard shortcuts work hand-in-hand.

Sketch of a computer mouse

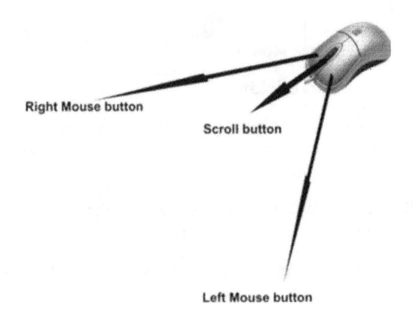

Right Mouse button

Scroll button

Left Mouse button

3. Mouse:

This is an oval-shaped portable input device with three buttons for scrolling, left clicking, and right clicking that enables work to be done effectively on a computer. The plural form of mouse is mice.

3.1 Types of Computer Mouse

- Mechanical Mouse.
- Optical Mechanical Mouse (Optomechanical).
- Laser Mouse.

- Optical Mouse.
- BlueTrack Mouse.

3.2 Forms of Clicking:

Left Clicking: This is the process of clicking the left side button of the mouse. It can also be called *clicking* without the addition of *left*.

Right Clicking: It is the process of clicking the right side button of a computer mouse.

Double Clicking: It is the process of clicking the left side button two times (twice) and immediately.

Triple Clicking: It is the process of clicking the left side button three times (thrice) and immediately.

Double clicking is used to select a word while triple clicking is used to select a sentence or paragraph.

Scroll Button: It is the little key attached to the mouse that looks like a tiny wheel. It takes you up and down a page when moved.

3.3 Mouse Pad: This is a small soft mat that is placed under the mouse to make it have a free movement.

3.4 Laptop Mouse Touchpad

This unlike the mouse we explained above is not external, rather it is inbuilt (comes with the laptop computer). With the presence of a laptop mouse touchpad, an external mouse is not needed to use a laptop, except in a case where it is malfunctioning or the operator prefers to use external one for some reasons.

The laptop mouse touchpad is usually positioned at the end of the keyboard section of a laptop computer. It is rectangular in shape with two buttons positioned below it. The two buttons/keys are used for left and right clicking just like the external mouse. Some laptops come with four mouse keys. Two placed above the mouse for left and right clicking and two other keys placed below it for the same function.

4. Definition Of Keyboard Shortcuts.

Keyboard shortcuts are defined as a series of keys, most times with combination that execute tasks which typically involve the use of mouse or other input devices.

5. Why You Should Use Shortcuts.

1. One may not be able to use a computer mouse easily because of disability or pain.

2. One may not be able to see the mouse pointer as a result of vision impairment, in such case what will the person do? The answer is SHORTCUT.

3. Research has made it known that Extensive mouse usage is related to Repetitive Syndrome Injury (RSI) greatly than the use of keyboard.

4. Keyboard shortcuts speed up computer users, making learning them a worthwhile effort.

5. When performing a job that requires precision, it is wise that you use the keyboard instead of mouse, for instance, if you are dealing with Text Editing, it is better you handle it using keyboard shortcuts than spending more time doing it with your computer mouse alone.

6. Studies calculate that using keyboard shortcuts allows working 10 times faster than working with the mouse. The time you spend looking for the mouse and then getting the cursor to the position you want is lost! Reducing your work duration by 10 times gives you greater results.

5.1 Ways To Become A Lover Of Shortcuts.

1. Always have the urge to learn new shortcut keys associated with the programs you use.
2. Be happy whenever you learn a new shortcut.

3. Try as much as you can to apply the new shortcuts you learnt.
4. Always bear it in mind that learning new shortcuts is worth it.
5. Always remember that the use of keyboard shortcuts keeps people healthy while performing computer activities.

5.2 How To Learn New Shortcut Keys

1. Do a research on them: quick references (a cheat sheet comprehensively compiled like ours) can go a long way to help you improve.
2. Buy applications that show you keyboard shortcuts every time you execute an action with mouse.
3. Disconnect your mouse if you must learn this fast.
4. Read user manuals and help topics (Whether offline or online).

5.3 Your Reward For Knowing Shortcut Keys.

1. You will get faster unimaginably.
2. Your level of efficiency will increase.
3. You will find it easy to use.
4. Opportunities are high that you will become an expert in what you do.
5. You won't have to go for **Office button**, click **New,** click **Blank and Recent**, and click **Create**

just to insert a fresh/blank page. **Ctrl +N** takes care of that in a second.

A Funny Note: Keyboarding and Mousing are in a marital union with Keyboarding being the head, so it will be unfair for anybody to put asunder between them.

5.4 Why We Emphasize On The Use of Shortcuts.

You may never leave your mouse completely unless you are ready to make your brain a box of keyboard shortcuts which will really be frustrating, just imagine yourself learning all shortcuts that go with the programs you use and their various versions. You shouldn't learn keyboard shortcuts that way.

Why we are emphasizing on the use of shortcuts is because mouse usage is becoming unusually common and unhealthy, too. So we just want to make sure both are combined so you can get fast, productive and healthy in your computer activities. All you need to know is just the most important ones associated with the programs you use.

CHAPTER 2.

15 (Fifteen) Special Keyboard Shortcuts.

The fifteen special keyboard shortcuts are fifteen (15) shortcuts every computer user should know.

The following is a list of keyboard shortcuts every computer user should know:

1. **Ctrl + A:** Control A, highlights or selects everything you have in the environment where you are working.

    *If you are like **"Wow, the content of this document is large and there is no time to select all of it, besides, it's going to mount pressure on my computer?"** Using the mouse for this is an outdated method of handling a task like selecting all, Ctrl+A will take care of that in a second.*

2. **Ctrl + C:** Control C copies any highlighted or selected element within the work environment.
   > *Saves the time and stress which would have been used to right click and click again just to copy. Use ctrl+c.*

3. **Ctrl + N:** Control N opens a new window or file.
   > *Instead of clicking* **File, New, blank/ template** *and another* **click,** *just press **Ctrl + N** and a fresh page or window will appear instantly.*

4. **Ctrl + O:** Control O opens a new program.
   > *Use ctrl +O when you want to locate / open a file or program.*

5. **Ctrl + P:** Control P prints the active document.
   > *Always use this to locate the printer dialog box, and thereafter print.*

6. **Ctrl + S:** Control S saves a new document or file and changes made by the user.
   > *Please stop! Don't use the mouse. Just press Ctrl+S and everything will be saved.*

7. **Ctrl +V:** Control V pastes copied elements into the active area of the program in use.

Using ctrl+V in a case like this Saves the time and stress of right clicking and clicking again just to paste.

8. **Ctrl + W:** Control W is used to close the page you are working on when you want to leave the work environment.

> **"There is a way Debby does this without using the mouse. Oh my God, why didn't I learn it then?"** Don't worry, I have the answer. Debby presses Ctrl+W to close active windows.

9. **Ctrl + X:** Control X cuts elements (making the elements to disappear from their original place). The difference between cutting and deleting elements is that in Cutting, what was cut doesn't get lost permanently but prepares itself so that it can be pasted on another location defined by the user.

> *Use ctrl+x when you think* **"this shouldn't be here and I can't stand the stress of retyping or redesigning it on the rightful place it belongs".**

10. **Ctrl + Y:** Control Y undoes already done actions.

> *Ctrl+Z brought back what you didn't need? Press Ctrl+ Y to remove it again.*

11. **Ctrl + Z:** Control Z redoes actions.

   Can't find what you typed now or a picture you inserted, it suddenly disappeared or you mistakenly removed it? Press Ctrl+Z to bring it back.

12. **Alt + F4:** Alternative F4 closes active windows or items.

   *You don't need to move the mouse in order to close an active window, just press **Alt + F4**. Also use it when you are done or you don't want somebody who is coming to see what you are doing.*

13. **Ctrl + F6:** Control F6 Navigates between open windows, making it possible for a user to see what is happening in windows that are active.

   Are you working in Microsoft Word and want to find out if the other active window where your browser is loading a page is still progressing? Use Ctrl + F6.

14. **F1:** This displays the help window.

   *Is your computer malfunctioning? Use **F1** to find help when you don't know what next to do.*

15. **F12:** This enables user to make changes to an already saved document.

> *F12 is the shortcut to use when you want to change the format in which you saved your existing document, password it, change its name, change the file location or destination, or make other changes to it. It will save you time.*

Note: The Control (Ctrl) key on Windows and Linux operating system is the same thing as Command (Cmmd) key on a Macintosh computer. So if you replace Control with Command key on a Mac computer for the special shortcuts listed above, you will get the same result.

CHAPTER 3.

Tips, and Keyboard Shortcuts for use in Adobe Photoshop.

About the program: Adobe Photoshop is a raster graphics editor developed, published, and sold by Adobe Systems Incorporated for MacOS and Windows operating systems.

A fresh topic ⌐

Download Photoshop CC.

Welcome to Photoshop CC! Whether you purchased a Complete, a Photography, or a Single-App plan, the process is the same. Simply download Photoshop from the adobe.com website and install it on your desktop.

1. Go to the <u>Creative Cloud apps catalog</u>. Locate Photoshop, and click **Download**.

If you are not signed in, you will be asked to sign in with your <u>Adobe ID</u> and password. Follow the onscreen instructions.

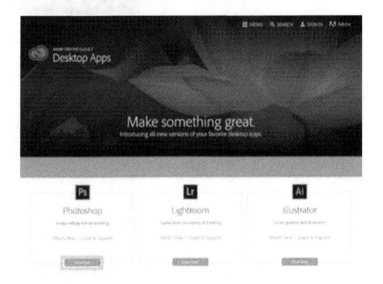

Note:

If you have a free trial membership to Creative Cloud, please refer to <u>Download and install a Creative Cloud trial</u>.

2. Your app begins to download.

At the same time, the Adobe Creative Cloud desktop app appears, and it will manage the rest of the installation process. Check your download progress in the status bar next to the app's name.

Note:

Depending on your network's speed, it could take some time to download your app.

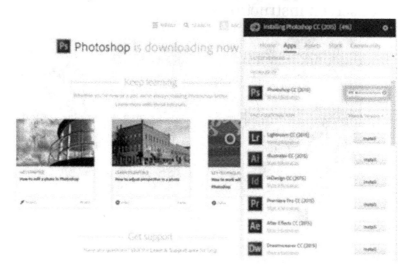

3. To launch your new app, find the Photoshop icon in the Apps panel and click Open.

   You can also launch Photoshop as you normally launch any app on your computer. Photoshop is installed in the same location where your applications are normally installed, such as the Program Files folder (Windows) or the Applications folder (Mac OS).

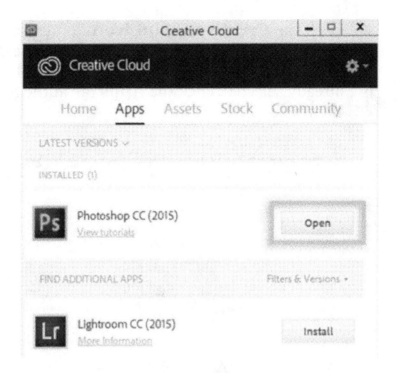

Note:

Having trouble with your first download? See Troubleshoot Creative Cloud download and installation issues.

Install Photoshop CS6.

You can download previous versions of Photoshop, such as CS6, directly from the Creative Cloud desktop app. You can have multiple versions of Photoshop installed on your computer at the same time, if you choose.

1. Click the **Creative Cloud icon**, located in the taskbar (Windows) or Apple menu bar (Mac OS), to open the Creative Cloud desktop app. If it's not already selected, click the **Apps** tab at the top of the window.

2. In the Find Additional Apps section, click **Filters & Versions** and choose **Previous Version**.

3. Find Photoshop in the list, and click the Install menu. Choose **CS6**.

   Photoshop CS6 downloads and is installed on your computer.

Note:

Previous product versions do not overwrite existing versions. You can have two versions of the same app running simultaneously on your computer, except for Acrobat XI (Windows) and Acrobat DC. Installation of these Acrobat versions will uninstall other versions of Acrobat.

End of Topic.

A fresh topic

Customize Keyboard Shortcuts.

Note:

In addition to using keyboard shortcuts, you can access many commands using context-sensitive menus that are relevant to the active tool, selection, or panel. To display a context-sensitive menu, right-click in the document window or panel.

Define New Keyboard Shortcuts

1. Do one of the following:
   o Choose Edit > Keyboard Shortcuts.
   o Choose Window > Workspace > Keyboard Shortcuts & Menus and click the Keyboard Shortcuts tab.
2. Choose a set of shortcuts from the Set menu at the top of the Keyboard Shortcuts & Menus dialog box.
3. Choose a shortcut type from the Shortcuts For menu:

Application Menus

Lets you customize keyboard shortcuts for items in the menu bar.

Panel Menus

Lets you customize keyboard shortcuts for items in panel menus.

Tools

Lets you customize keyboard shortcuts for tools in the toolbox.

4. In the Shortcut column of the scroll list, select the shortcut you want to modify.
5. Type a new shortcut.

If the keyboard shortcut is already assigned to another command or tool in the set, an alert appears. Click Accept to assign the shortcut to the new command or tool and erase the previously assigned shortcut. After you reassign a shortcut, you can click Undo Changes to undo the change, or click Accept and Go To Conflict to assign a new shortcut to the other command or tool.

6. When you're finished changing shortcuts, do one of the following:
    o To save all changes to the current set of keyboard shortcuts, click the Save Set button 🖫. Changes to a custom set are saved. If you're saving changes to the Photoshop Defaults set, the Save dialog box opens. Enter a name for the new set and click Save.
    o To create a new set based on the current set of shortcuts, click the Save Set As button 🖫 . In the Save dialog box, enter a name for the new set in the Name text box, and click Save. The new keyboard shortcut set will appear in the pop-up menu under the new name.
    o To discard the last saved change without closing the dialog box, click Undo.
    o To return a new shortcut to the default, click Use Default.
    o To discard all changes and exit the dialog box, click Cancel.

Note:

If you haven't saved the current set of changes, you can click Cancel to discard all changes and exit the dialog box.

Clear shortcuts from a command or tool

1. Choose Edit > Keyboard Shortcuts.
2. In the Keyboard Shortcuts dialog box, select the command or tool name whose shortcut you want to delete.
3. Click Delete Shortcut.

Delete a set of shortcuts

1. Choose Edit > Keyboard Shortcuts.
2. In the Set pop-up menu, choose the shortcut set that you want to delete.
3. Click the Delete icon 🗑 and then click OK to exit the dialog box.

View a list of current shortcuts

To view a list of current shortcuts, export them to an HTML file, which you can display or print with a web browser.

1. Choose Edit > Keyboard Shortcuts.
2. From the Shortcuts For menu, choose a shortcut type: Application Menus, Panel Menus, or Tools.

3. Click Summarize.

End of Topic.

A fresh topic ⌐└▶

Default Keyboard Shortcuts in Adobe Photoshop.

Use the following list of keyboard shortcuts to enhance your productivity in Adobe Photoshop.

Keys for Invoking Search Experience.

Result	Windows Shortcut	Mac OS Shortcut
Search across Photoshop UI, Help & Learn content, and Adobe Stock assets.	Control + F	Command + F

Function Keys

Result	Windows	Mac OS
Start Help	F1	Help key
Undo/Redo		F1
Cut	F2	F2
Copy	F3	F3
Paste	F4	F4
Show/Hide Brush panel	F5	F5
Show/Hide Color panel	F6	F6
Show/Hide Layers panel	F7	F7
Show/Hide Info panel	F8	F8
Show/Hide Actions panel	F9	Option + F9
Revert	F12	F12
Fill	Shift + F5	Shift + F5
Feather Selection	Shift + F6	Shift + F6
Inverse Selection	Shift + F7	Shift + F7

Keys for Selecting Tools.

Holding down a key temporarily activates a tool. Letting go of the key returns to the previous tool.

Note:

In rows with multiple tools, repeatedly press the same shortcut to toggle through the group.

Result	Windows Shortcut	Mac OS Shortcut
Cycle through tools with the	Shift-press shortcut key (if Use Shift Key for	Shift-press shortcut key (if Use Shift Key for

same shortcut key	Tool Switch preference is selected)	Tool Switch preference is selected)
Cycle through hidden tools	Alt-click + tool (except Add Anchor Point, Delete Anchor Point, and Convert Point tools)	Option-click + tool (except Add Anchor Point, Delete Anchor Point, and Convert Point tools)
Move tool	V	V
Rectangular Marquee tool† Elliptical Marquee tool	M	M
Lasso tool Polygonal Lasso tool Magnetic Lasso tool	L	L
Magic Wand tool Quick Selection tool	W	W
Crop tool Slice tool	C	C

Slice Select tool		
Eyedropper tool[†] Color Sampler tool Ruler tool Note tool Count tool[*]	I	I
Spot Healing Brush tool Healing Brush tool Patch tool Red Eye tool	J	J
Brush tool Pencil tool Color Replacement tool Mixer Brush tool	B	B

Clone Stamp tool Pattern Stamp tool	S	S
History Brush tool Art History Brush tool	Y	Y
Eraser tool[†] Background Eraser tool Magic Eraser tool	E	E
Gradient tool Paint Bucket tool	G	G
Dodge tool Burn tool Sponge tool	O	O
Pen tool Freeform Pen tool	P	P

Horizontal Type tool Vertical Type tool Horizontal Type mask tool Vertical Type mask tool	T	T
Path Selection tool Direct Selection tool	A	A
Rectangle tool Rounded Rectangle tool Ellipse tool Polygon tool Line tool Custom Shape tool	U	U
3D Object Rotate tool*	K	K

3D Object Roll tool* 3D Object Pan tool* 3D Object Slide tool* 3D Object Scale tool*		
3D Camera Rotate tool* 3D Camera Roll tool* 3D Camera Pan tool* 3D Camera Walk tool* 3D Camera Zoom*	N	N
Hand tool[†]	H	H
Rotate View tool	R	R
Zoom tool[†]	Z	Z
[†]Use same shortcut key for Liquify *Photoshop Extended only		

This partial list provides shortcuts that don't appear in menu commands or tool tips.

Result	Windows Shortcut	Mac OS Shortcut
Cycle through open documents	Control + Tab	Control + Tab
Switch to previous document	Shift + Control + Tab	Shift + Command + `(grave accent)
Close a file in Photoshop and open Bridge	Shift-Control-W	Shift-Command-W
Toggle between Standard mode and Quick Mask mode	Q	Q
Toggle (forward) between Standard screen mode, Full screen mode with menu bar, and Full screen mode	F	F
Toggle (backward) between Standard screen mode, Full screen mode with menu bar, and Full screen mode	Shift + F	Shift + F

Toggle (forward) canvas color	Spacebar + F (or right-click canvas background and select color)	Spacebar + F (or Control-click canvas background and select color)
Toggle (backward) canvas color	Spacebar + Shift + F	Spacebar + Shift + F
Fit image in window	Double-click Hand tool	Double-click Hand tool
Magnify 100%	Double-click Zoom tool or Ctrl + 1	Double-click Zoom tool or Command + 1
Switch to Hand tool (when not in text-edit mode)	Spacebar	Spacebar
Simultaneously pan multiple documents with Hand tool	Shift-drag	Shift-drag
Switch to Zoom In tool	Control + spacebar	Command + spacebar
Switch to Zoom Out tool	Alt + spacebar	Option + spacebar
Move Zoom marquee while dragging with the Zoom tool	Spacebar-drag	Spacebar-drag
Apply zoom percentage, and	Shift + Enter in Navigator	Shift + Return in Navigator

keep zoom percentage box active	panel zoom percentage box	panel zoom percentage box
Zoom in on specified area of an image	Control-drag over preview in Navigator panel	Command-drag over preview in Navigator panel
Temporarily zoom into an image	Hold down H and then click in the image and hold down the mouse button	Hold down H and then click in the image and hold down the mouse button
Scroll image with Hand tool	Spacebar-drag, or drag view area box in Navigator panel	Spacebar-drag, or drag view area box in Navigator panel
Scroll up or down 1 screen	Page Up or Page Down[†]	Page Up or Page Down[†]
Scroll up or down 10 units	Shift + Page Up or Page Down[†]	Shift + Page Up or Page Down[†]
Move view to upper-left corner or lower-right corner	Home or End	Home or End
Toggle layer mask on/off as rubylith	\ (backslash)	\ (backslash)

(layer mask must be selected)		
†Hold down Ctrl (Windows) or Command (Mac OS) to scroll left (Page Up) or right (Page Down)		

Keys for Puppet Warp.

This partial list provides shortcuts that don't appear in menu commands or tool tips.

Result	Windows Shortcut	Mac OS Shortcut
Cancel completely	Esc	Esc
Undo last pin adjustment	Ctrl + Z	Command + Z
Select all pins	Ctrl + A	Command + A
Deselect all pins	Ctrl + D	Command + D
Select multiple pins	Shift-click	Shift-click
Move multiple selected pins	Shift-drag	Shift-drag
Temporarily hide pins	H	H

Keys for Refine Edge.

Result	Windows Shortcut	Mac OS Shortcut
Open the Refine Edge dialog box	Control + Alt + R	Command + Option + R
Cycle (forward) through preview modes	F	F
Cycle (backward) through preview modes	Shift + F	Shift + F
Toggle between original image and selection preview	X	X
Toggle between original selection and refined version	P	P
Toggle radius preview on and off	J	J
Toggle between Refine Radius and Erase Refinements tools	Shift + E	Shift + E

Keys for the Filter Gallery.

Result	Windows Shortcut	Mac OS Shortcut
Apply a new filter on top of selected	Alt-click a filter	Option-click a filter

Reapply last-used filter	Control + Alt + F	Command + Alt + F
Open/close all disclosure triangles	Alt-click a disclosure triangle	Option-click a disclosure triangle
Change Cancel button to Default	Control	Command
Change Cancel button to Reset	Alt	Option
Undo/Redo	Control + Z	Command + Z
Step forward	Control + Shift + Z	Command + Shift + Z
Step backward	Control + Alt + Z	Command + Option + Z

Keys for Liquify.

Result	Windows Shortcut	Mac OS Shortcut
Forward Warp tool	W	W
Reconstruct tool	R	R
Twirl Clockwise tool	C	C
Pucker tool	S	S
Bloat tool	B	B
Push Left tool	O	O
Mirror tool	M	M
Turbulence tool	T	T
Freeze Mask tool	F	F

Thaw Mask tool	D	D
Reverse direction for Bloat, Pucker, Push Left, and Mirror tools	Alt + tool	Option + tool
Continually sample the distortion	Alt-drag in preview with Reconstruct tool, Displace, Amplitwist, or Affine mode selected	Option-drag in preview with Reconstruct tool, Displace, Amplitwist, or Affine mode selected
Decrease/increase brush size by 2, or density, pressure, rate, or turbulent jitter by 1	Down Arrow/Up Arrow in Brush Size, Density, Pressure, Rate, or Turbulent Jitter text box[†]	Down Arrow/Up Arrow in Brush Size, Density, Pressure, Rate, or Turbulent Jitter text box[†]
Decrease/increase brush size by 2, or density, pressure, rate, or turbulent jitter by 1	Left Arrow/Right Arrow with Brush Size, Density, Pressure, Rate, or Turbulent	Left Arrow/Right Arrow with Brush Size, Density, Pressure, Rate, or Turbulent

	Jitter slider showing[†]	Jitter slider showing[†]
Cycle through controls on right from top	Tab	Tab
Cycle through controls on right from bottom	Shift + Tab	Shift + Tab
Change Cancel to Reset	Alt	Option
[†]Hold down Shift to decrease/increase by 10		

Keys for Vanishing Point.

Result	Windows Shortcut	Mac OS Shortcut
Zoom 2x (temporary)	X	X
Zoom in	Control + + (plus)	Command + + (plus)
Zoom out	Control + - (hyphen)	Command + - (hyphen)
Fit in view	Control + 0 (zero), Double-click Hand tool	Command + 0 (zero), Double-click Hand tool
Zoom to center at 100%	Double-click Zoom tool	Double-click Zoom tool

Increase brush size (Brush, Stamp tools)	]	]
Decrease brush size (Brush, Stamp tools)	[	[
Increase brush hardness (Brush, Stamp tools)	Shift +]	Shift +]
Decrease brush hardness (Brush, Stamp tools)	Shift + [	Shift + [
Undo last action	Control + Z	Command + Z
Redo last action	Control + Shift + Z	Command + Shift + Z
Deselect all	Control + D	Command + D
Hide selection and planes	Control + H	Command + H
Move selection 1 pixel	Arrow keys	Arrow keys
Move selection 10 pixels	Shift + arrow keys	Shift + arrow keys
Copy	Control + C	Command + C
Paste	Control + V	Command + V
Repeat last duplicate and move	Control + Shift + T	Command + Shift + T
Create a floating selection from the current selection	Control + Alt + T	

Fill a selection with image under the pointer	Control-drag	Command-drag
Create a duplicate of the selection as a floating selection	Control + Alt-drag	Command + Option-drag
Constrain selection to a 15° rotation	Alt + Shift to rotate	Option + Shift to rotate
Select a plane under another selected plane	Control-click the plane	Command-click the plane
Create 90 degree plane off parent plane	Control-drag	Command-drag
Delete last node while creating plane	Backspace	Delete
Make a full canvas plane, square to the camera	Double-click the Create Plane tool	Double-click the Create Plane tool
Show/hide measurements (Photoshop Extended only)	Control + Shift + H	Command + Shift + H
Export to a DFX file (Photoshop Extended only)	Control + E	Command + E
Export to a 3DS file (Photoshop Extended only)	Control + Shift + E	Command + Shift + E

Keys for the Camera Raw Dialog Box.

Note:

Holding down a key temporarily activates a tool. Letting go of the key returns to the previous tool.

Result	Windows Shortcut	Mac OS Shortcut
Zoom tool	Z	Z
Hand tool	H	H
White Balance tool	I	I
Color Sampler tool	S	S
Crop tool	C	C
Straighten tool	A	A
Spot Removal tool	B	B
Red Eye Removal tool	E	E
Basic panel	Ctrl + Alt + 1	Command + Option + 1
Tone Curve panel	Ctrl + Alt + 2	Command + Option + 2
Detail panel	Ctrl + Alt + 3	Command + Option + 3
HSL/Grayscale panel	Ctrl + Alt + 4	Command + Option + 4
Split Toning panel	Ctrl + Alt + 5	Command + Option + 5
Lens Corrections panel	Ctrl + Alt + 6	Command + Option + 6

Camera Calibration panel	Ctrl + Alt + 7	Command + Option + 7
Presets panel	Ctrl + Alt + 9	Command + Option + 9 (Mac OS Universal Access zoom shortcut must be disabled in System Preferences)
Open Snapshots panel	Ctrl + Alt + 9	Command + Option + 9
Parametric Curve Targeted Adjustment tool	Ctrl + Alt + Shift + T	Command + Option + Shift + T
Hue Targeted Adjustment tool	Ctrl + Alt + Shift + H	Command + Option + Shift + H
Saturation Targeted Adjustment tool	Ctrl + Alt + Shift + S	Command + Option + Shift + S
Luminance Targeted Adjustment tool	Ctrl + Alt + Shift + L	Command + Option + Shift + L
Grayscale Mix Targeted Adjustment tool	Ctrl + Alt + Shift + G	Command + Option + Shift + G
Last-used Targeted Adjustment tool	T	T

Adjustment Brush tool	K	K
Graduated Filter tool	G	G
Increase/decrease brush size	] / [	] / [
Increase/decrease brush feather	Shift +] / Shift + [	Shift +] / Shift + [
Increase/decrease Adjustment Brush tool flow in increments of 10	= (equal sign) / - (hyphen)	= (equal sign) / - (hyphen)
Temporarily switch from Add to Erase mode for the Adjustment Brush tool, or from Erase to Add mode	Alt	Option
Increase/decrease temporary Adjustment Brush tool size	Alt +] / Alt + [	Option +] / Option + [
Increase/decrease temporary Adjustment Brushtool feather	Alt + Shift +] / Alt + Shift + [	Option + Shift +] / Option + Shift + [
Increase/decrease temporary Adjustment Brush tool flow in increments of 10	Alt + = (equal sign) / Alt + - (hyphen)	Option = (equal sign) / Option + - (hyphen)

Switch to New mode from Add or Erase mode of the Adjustment Brush tool or the Graduated Filter	N	N
Toggle Auto Mask for Adjustment Brush tool	M	M
Toggle Show Mask for Adjustment Brush tool	Y	Y
Toggle pins for Adjustment Brush tool	V	V
Toggle overlay for Graduated Filter, Spot Removal tool, or Red Eye Removal tool.	V	V
Rotate image left	L or Ctrl +]	L or Command +]
Rotate image right	R or Ctrl + [	R or Command + [
Zoom in	Ctrl + + (plus)	Command + + (plus)
Zoom out	Ctrl + - (hyphen)	Command + - (hyphen)
Temporarily switch to Zoom In tool	Ctrl	Command

(Doesn't work when Straighten tool is selected. If Crop tool is active, temporarily switches to Straighten tool.)		
Temporarily switch to Zoom Out tool and change the Open Image button to Open Copy and the Cancel button to Reset.	Alt	Option
Toggle preview	P	P
Full screen mode	F	F
Temporarily activate the White Balance tool and change the Open Image button to Open Object. (Does not work if Crop tool is active)	Shift	Shift
Select multiple points in Curves panel	Click the first point; Shift-click additional points	Click the first point; Shift-click additional points
Add point to curve in Curves panel	Control-click in preview	Command-click in preview

Move selected point in Curves panel (1 unit)	Arrow keys	Arrow keys
Move selected point in Curves panel (10 units)	Shift-arrow	Shift-arrow
Open selected images in Camera Raw dialog box from Bridge	Ctrl + R	Command + R
Open selected images from Bridge bypassing Camera Raw dialog box	Shift + double-click image	Shift + double-click image
Display highlights that will be clipped in Preview	Alt-drag Exposure, Recovery, or Black sliders	Option-drag Exposure, Recovery, or Black sliders
Highlight clipping warning	O	O
Shadows clipping warning	U	U
(Filmstrip mode) Add 1 - 5 star rating	Ctrl +1 - 5	Command + 1 - 5
(Filmstrip mode) Increase/decrease rating	Ctrl +. (period) / Ctrl+, (comma)	Command + . (period) / Command+, (comma)
(Filmstrip mode) Add red label	Ctrl + 6	Command + 6

(Filmstrip mode) Add yellow label	Ctrl + 7	Command + 7
(Filmstrip mode) Add green label	Ctrl + 8	Command + 8
(Filmstrip mode) Add blue label	Ctrl + 9	Command + 9
(Filmstrip mode) Add purple label	Ctrl + Shift + 0	Command + Shift + 0
Camera Raw preferences	Ctrl + K	Command + K
Deletes Adobe Camera Raw preferences	Ctrl + Alt (on open)	Option + Shift (on open)

Keys for the Black-and-White Dialog Box.

Result	Windows Shortcut	Mac OS Shortcut
Open the Black-and-White dialog box	Shift + Control + Alt + B	Shift + Command + Option+ B
Increase/decrease selected value by 1%	Up Arrow/Down Arrow	Up Arrow/Down Arrow
Increase/decrease selected value by 10%	Shift + Up Arrow/Down Arrow	Shift + Up Arrow/Down Arrow

Change the values of the closest color slider	Click-drag on the image	Click-drag on the image

Keys for Curves.

Result	Windows Shortcut	Mac OS Shortcut
Open the Curves dialog box	Control + M	Command + M
Select next point on the curve	+ (plus)	+ (plus)
Select the previous point on the curve	– (minus)	– (minus)
Select multiple points on the curve	Shift-click the points	Shift-click the points
Deselect a point	Control + D	Command + D
To delete a point on the curve	Select a point and press Delete	Select a point and press Delete
Move the selected point 1 unit	Arrow keys	Arrow keys
Move the selected point 10 units	Shift + Arrow keys	Shift + Arrow keys

Display highlights and shadows that will be clipped	Alt-drag black/white point sliders	Option-drag black/white point sliders
Set a point to the composite curve	Control-click the image	Command-click the image
Set a point to the channel curves	Shift + Control-click the image	Shift + Command-click the image
Toggle grid size	Alt-click the field	Option-click the field

Keys for Selecting and Moving Objects.

This partial list provides shortcuts that don't appear in menu commands or tool tips.

Result	Windows Shortcut	Mac OS Shortcut
Reposition marquee while selecting‡	Any marquee tool (except single column and single row) + spacebar-drag	Any marquee tool (except single column and single row) + spacebar-drag
Add to a selection	Any selection tool + Shift-drag	Any selection tool + Shift-drag

Subtract from a selection	Any selection tool + Alt-drag	Any selection tool + Option-drag
Intersect a selection	Any selection tool (except Quick Selection tool) + Shift-Alt-drag	Any selection tool (except Quick Selection tool) + Shift-Option-drag
Constrain marquee to square or circle (if no other selections are active)[‡]	Shift-drag	Shift-drag
Draw marquee from center (if no other selections are active)[‡]	Alt-drag	Option-drag
Constrain shape and draw marquee from center[‡]	Shift + Alt-drag	Shift + Option-drag
Switch to Move tool	Control (except when Hand, Slice, Path, Shape, or any Pen tool is selected)	Command (except when Hand, Slice, Path, Shape, or any Pen tool is selected)
Switch from Magnetic Lasso tool to Lasso tool	Alt-drag	Option-drag
Switch from Magnetic Lasso tool	Alt-click	Option-click

to polygonal Lasso tool		
Apply/cancel an operation of the Magnetic Lasso	Enter/Esc or Control + . (period)	Return/Esc or Command + . (period)
Move copy of selection	Move tool + Alt-drag selection[‡]	Move tool + Option-drag selection[‡]
Move selection area 1 pixel	Any selection + Right Arrow, Left Arrow, Up Arrow, or Down Arrow[†]	Any selection + Right Arrow, Left Arrow, Up Arrow, or Down Arrow[†]
Move selection 1 pixel	Move tool + Right Arrow, Left Arrow, Up Arrow, or Down Arrow[†‡]	Move tool + Right Arrow, Left Arrow, Up Arrow, or Down Arrow[†‡]
Move layer 1 pixel when nothing selected on layer	Control + Right Arrow, Left Arrow, Up Arrow, or Down Arrow[†]	Command + Right Arrow, Left Arrow, Up Arrow, or Down Arrow[†]
Increase/decrease detection width	Magnetic Lasso tool + [or]	Magnetic Lasso tool + [or]
Accept cropping or exit cropping	Crop tool + Enter or Esc	Crop tool + Return or Esc
Toggle crop shield off and on	/ (forward slash)	/ (forward slash)

Make protractor	Ruler tool + Alt-drag end point	Ruler tool + Option-drag end point
Snap guide to ruler ticks (except when View > Snap is unchecked)	Shift-drag guide	Shift-drag guide
Convert between horizontal and vertical guide	Alt-drag guide	Option-drag guide
[†]Hold down Shift to move 10 pixels [‡]Applies to shape tools		

Keys for Transforming Selections, Selection Borders, and Paths.

This partial list provides shortcuts that don't appear in menu commands or tool tips.

Result	Windows Shortcut	Mac OS Shortcut
Transform from center or reflect	Alt	Option
Constrain	Shift	Shift
Distort	Control	Command
Apply	Enter	Return
Cancel	Control + . (period) or Esc	Command + . (period) or Esc

Free transform with duplicate data	Control + Alt + T	Command + Option + T
Transform again with duplicate data	Control + Shift + Alt + T	Command + Shift + Option + T

Keys for Editing Paths.

This partial list provides shortcuts that don't appear in menu commands or tool tips.

Result	Windows Shortcut	Mac OS Shortcut
Select multiple anchor points	Direct selection tool + Shift-click	Direct selection tool + Shift-click
Select entire path	Direct selection tool + Alt-click	Direct selection tool + Option-click
Duplicate a path	Pen (any Pen tool), Path Selection or Direct Selection tool + Control + Alt-drag	Pen (any Pen tool), Path Selection or Direct Selection tool + Command + Option-drag
Switch from Path Selection, Pen, Add Anchor	Control	Command

Point, Delete Anchor Point, or Convert Point tools to Direct Selection tool		
Switch from Pen tool or Freeform Pen tool to Convert Point tool when pointer is over anchor or direction point	Alt	Option
Close path	Magnetic Pen tool-double-click	Magnetic Pen tool-double-click
Close path with straight-line segment	Magnetic Pen tool + Alt-double-click	Magnetic Pen tool + Option-double-click

Keys For Painting.

This partial list provides shortcuts that don't appear in menu commands or tool tips.

Result	Windows Shortcut	Mac OS Shortcut
Select foreground	Any painting tool + Shift + Alt +	Any painting tool + Control + Option +

color from color picker	right-click and drag	Command and drag
Select foreground color from image with Eyedropper tool	Any painting tool + Alt or any shape tool + Alt (except when Paths option is selected)	Any painting tool + Option or any shape tool + Option (except when Paths option is selected)
Select background color	Eyedropper tool + Alt-click	Eyedropper tool + Option-click
Color sampler tool	Eyedropper tool + Shift	Eyedropper tool + Shift
Deletes color sampler	Color sampler tool + Alt-click	Color sampler tool + Option-click
Sets opacity, tolerance, strength, or exposure for painting mode	Any painting or editing tool + number keys (e.g., 0 = 100%, 1 = 10%, 4 then 5 in quick succession = 45%) (when airbrush option is enabled, use Shift + number keys)	Any painting or editing tool + number keys (e.g., 0 = 100%, 1 = 10%, 4 then 5 in quick succession = 45%) (when airbrush option is enabled, use Shift + number keys)
Sets flow for painting mode	Any painting or editing tool + Shift + number	Any painting or editing tool + Shift + number

	keys (e.g., 0 = 100%, 1 = 10%, 4 then 5 in quick succession = 45%) (when airbrush option is enabled, omit Shift)	keys (e.g., 0 = 100%, 1 = 10%, 4 then 5 in quick succession = 45%) (when airbrush option is enabled, omit Shift)
Mixer Brush changes Mix setting	Alt + Shift + number	Option + Shift + number
Mixer Brush changes Wet setting	Number keys	Number keys
Mixer Brush changes Wet and Mix to zero	00	00
Cycle through blending modes	Shift + + (plus) or – (minus)	Shift + + (plus) or – (minus)
Open Fill dialog box on background or standard layer	Backspace or Shift + Backspace	Delete or Shift + Delete
Fill with foreground or background color	Alt + Backspace or Control + Backspace[†]	Option + Delete or Command + Delete[†]

Fill from history	Control + Alt + Backspace[†]	Command + Option + Delete[†]
Displays Fill dialog box	Shift + Backspace	Shift + Delete
Lock transparent pixels on/off	/ (forward slash)	/ (forward slash)
Connects points with a straight line	Any painting tool + Shift-click	Any painting tool + Shift-click
[†]Hold down Shift to preserve transparency		

Keys For Blending Modes.

Result	Windows Shortcut	Mac OS Shortcut
Cycle through blending modes	Shift + + (plus) or − (minus)	Shift + + (plus) or − (minus)
Normal	Shift + Alt + N	Shift + Option + N
Dissolve	Shift + Alt + I	Shift + Option + I
Behind (Brush tool only)	Shift + Alt + Q	Shift + Option + Q
Clear (Brush tool only)	Shift + Alt + R	Shift + Option + R
Darken	Shift + Alt + K	Shift + Option + K

Multiply	Shift + Alt + M	Shift + Option + M
Color Burn	Shift + Alt + B	Shift + Option + B
Linear Burn	Shift + Alt + A	Shift + Option + A
Lighten	Shift + Alt + G	Shift + Option + G
Screen	Shift + Alt + S	Shift + Option + S
Color Dodge	Shift + Alt + D	Shift + Option + D
Linear Dodge	Shift + Alt + W	Shift + Option + W
Overlay	Shift + Alt + O	Shift + Option + O
Soft Light	Shift + Alt + F	Shift + Option + F
Hard Light	Shift + Alt + H	Shift + Option + H
Vivid Light	Shift + Alt + V	Shift + Option + V
Linear Light	Shift + Alt + J	Shift + Option + J
Pin Light	Shift + Alt + Z	Shift + Option + Z
Hard Mix	Shift + Alt + L	Shift + Option + L
Difference	Shift + Alt + E	Shift + Option + E

Exclusion	Shift + Alt + X	Shift + Option + X
Hue	Shift + Alt + U	Shift + Option + U
Saturation	Shift + Alt + T	Shift + Option + T
Color	Shift + Alt + C	Shift + Option + C
Luminosity	Shift + Alt + Y	Shift + Option + Y
Desaturate	Sponge tool + Shift + Alt + D	Sponge tool + Shift + Option + D
Saturate	Sponge tool + Shift + Alt + S	Sponge tool + Shift + Option + S
Dodge/burn shadows	Dodge tool/Burn tool + Shift + Alt + S	Dodge tool/Burn tool + Shift + Option + S
Dodge/burn midtones	Dodge tool/Burn tool + Shift + Alt + M	Dodge tool/Burn tool + Shift + Option + M
Dodge/burn highlights	Dodge tool/Burn tool + Shift + Alt + H	Dodge tool/Burn tool + Shift + Option + H
Set blending mode to Threshold for bitmap images,	Shift + Alt + N	Shift + Option + N

Normal for all other images		

Keys for Selecting and Editing Text.

This partial list provides shortcuts that don't appear in menu commands or tool tips.

Result	Windows Shortcut	Mac OS Shortcut
Move type in image	Control-drag type when Type layer is selected	Command-drag type when Type layer is selected
Select 1 character left/right or 1 line down/up, or 1 word left/right	Shift + Left Arrow/Right Arrow or Down Arrow/Up Arrow, or Control + Shift + Left Arrow/Right Arrow	Shift + Left Arrow/Right Arrow or Down Arrow/Up Arrow, or Command + Shift + Left Arrow/Right Arrow
Select characters from insertion point to mouse click point	Shift-click	Shift-click
Move 1 character left/right, 1 line down/up, or 1 word left/right	Left Arrow/Right Arrow, Down Arrow/Up	Left Arrow/Right Arrow, Down Arrow/Up

	Arrow, or Control + Left Arrow/Right Arrow	Arrow, or Command + Left Arrow/Right Arrow
Create a new text layer, when a text layer is selected in the Layers panel	Shift-click	Shift-click
Select a word, line, paragraph, or story	Double-click, triple-click, quadruple-click, or quintuple-click	Double-click, triple-click, quadruple-click, or quintuple-click
Show/Hide selection on selected type	Control + H	Command + H
Display the bounding box for transforming text when editing text, or activate Move tool if cursor is inside the bounding box	Control	Command
Scale text within a bounding box when resizing	Control-drag a bounding box handle	Command-drag a bounding box handle

the bounding box		
Move text box while creating text box	Spacebar-drag	Spacebar-drag

Keys for Formatting Type.

This partial list provides shortcuts that don't appear in menu commands or tool tips.

Result	Windows Shortcut	Mac OS Shortcut
Align left, center, or right	Horizontal Type tool + Control + Shift + L, C, or R	Horizontal Type tool + Command + Shift + L, C, or R
Align top, center, or bottom	Vertical Type tool + Control + Shift + L, C, or R	Vertical Type tool + Command + Shift + L, C, or R
Choose 100% horizontal scale	Control + Shift + X	Command + Shift + X
Choose 100% vertical scale	Control + Shift + Alt + X	Command + Shift + Option + X

Choose Auto leading	Control + Shift + Alt + A	Command + Shift + Option + A
Choose 0 for tracking	Control + Shift + Q	Command + Control + Shift + Q
Justify paragraph, left aligns last line	Control + Shift + J	Command + Shift + J
Justify paragraph, justifies all	Control + Shift + F	Command + Shift + F
Toggle paragraph hyphenation on/off	Control + Shift + Alt + H	Command + Control + Shift + Option + H
Toggle single/every-line composer on/off	Control + Shift + Alt + T	Command + Shift + Option + T
Decrease or increase type size of selected text 2 points or pixels	Control + Shift + < or >[†]	Command + Shift + < or >[†]
Decrease or increase leading 2 points or pixels	Alt + Down Arrow or Up Arrow[††]	Option + Down Arrow or Up Arrow[††]
Decrease or increase baseline shift 2 points or pixels	Shift + Alt + Down Arrow or Up Arrow[††]	Shift + Option + Down Arrow or Up Arrow[††]
Decrease or increase kerning/tracking 20/1000 ems	Alt + Left Arrow or Right Arrow[††]	Option + Left Arrow or Right Arrow[††]

69

†Hold down Alt (Win) or Option (macOS) to decrease/increase by 10	
††Hold down Ctrl (Windows) or Command (macOS) to decrease/increase by 10	

Keys for Slicing and Optimizing.

Result	Windows Shortcut	Mac OS Shortcut
Toggle between Slice tool and Slice Selection tool	Control	Command
Draw square slice	Shift-drag	Shift-drag
Draw from center outward	Alt-drag	Option-drag
Draw square slice from center outward	Shift + Alt-drag	Shift + Option-drag
Reposition slice while creating slice	Spacebar-drag	Spacebar-drag
Open context-sensitive menu	Right-click slice	Control-click slice

Keys for using Panels.

This partial list provides shortcuts that don't appear in menu commands or tool tips.

Result	Windows Shortcut	Mac OS Shortcut

	Alt-click New button	Option-click New button
Set options for new items (except for Actions, Animation, Styles, Brushes, Tool Presets, and Layer Comps panels)	Alt-click New button	Option-click New button
Delete without confirmation (except for the Brush panel)	Alt-click Delete button	Option-click Delete button
Apply value and keep text box active	Shift + Enter	Shift + Return
Show/Hide all panels	Tab	Tab
Show/Hide all panels except the toolbox and options bar	Shift + Tab	Shift + Tab
Highlight options bar	Select tool and press Enter	Select tool and press Return
Increase/decrease selected values by 10	Shift + Up Arrow/Down Arrow	Shift + Up Arrow/Down Arrow

Result	Windows Shortcut	Mac OS Shortcut
Turn command on and all others off, or	Alt-click the check mark next to a command	Option-click the check mark next to a command

turn all commands on		
Turn current modal control on and toggle all other modal controls	Alt-click	Option-click
Change action or action set options	Alt + double-click action or action set	Option + double-click action or action set
Display Options dialog box for recorded command	Double-click recorded command	Double-click recorded command
Play entire action	Control + double-click an action	Command + double-click an action
Collapse/expand all components of an action	Alt-click the triangle	Option-click the triangle
Play a command	Control-click the Play button	Command-click the Play button
Create new action and begin recording without confirmation	Alt-click the New Action button	Option-click the New Action button

Select contiguous items of the same kind	Shift-click the action/command	Shift-click the action/command
Select discontiguous items of the same kind	Control-click the action/command	Command-click the action/command

Keys for Adjustment Layers

Note:

If you prefer channel shortcuts starting with Alt/Option + 1 for red, choose Edit > Keyboard Shortcuts, and select Use Legacy Channel Shortcuts. Then restart Photoshop.

Result	Windows Shortcut	Mac OS Shortcut
Choose specific channel for adjustment	Alt + 3 (red), 4 (green), 5 (blue)	Option + 3 (red), 4 (green), 5 (blue)
Choose composite channel for adjustment	Alt + 2	Option + 2
Delete adjustment layer	Delete or Backspace	Delete

Define Auto options for Levels or Curves	Alt-click Auto button	Option-click Auto button

Keys for the Animation panel in Frames Mode.

Result	Windows Shortcut	Mac OS Shortcut
Select/deselect multiple contiguous frames	Shift-click second frame	Shift-click second frame
Select/deselect multiple discontiguous frames	Control-click multiple frames	Command-click multiple frames
Paste using previous settings without displaying the dialog box	Alt + Paste Frames command from the Panel pop-up menu	Option + Paste Frames command from the Panel pop-up menu

Keys for the Animation Panel in Timeline Mode (Photoshop Extended).

Note:

To enable all shortcuts, choose Enable Timeline Shortcut Keys from the Animation (Timeline) panel menu.

Result	Windows Shortcut	Mac OS Shortcut
Start playing the timeline or Animation panel	Spacebar	Spacebar
Switch between timecode and frame numbers (current time view)	Alt + click the current-time display in the upper-left corner of the timeline.	Option + click the current-time display in the upper-left corner of the timeline.
Expand and collapse list of layers	Alt + click	Option + click on list triangles
Jump to the next/previous whole second in timeline	Hold down the Shift key when clicking the Next/Previous Frame buttons (on either side of the Play button).	Hold down the Shift key when clicking the Next/Previous Frame buttons (on either side of the Play button)
Increase playback speed	Hold down the Shift key while dragging the current time.	Hold down the Shift key while dragging the current time.

Decrease playback speed	Hold down the Control key while dragging the current time.	Hold down the Command key while dragging the current time.
Snap an object (keyframe, the current time, layer in point, and so on) to the nearest object in timeline	Shift-drag	Shift-drag
Scale (evenly distribute to condensed or extended length) a selected group of multiple keyframes	Alt-drag (first or last keyframe in the selection)	Option-drag (first or last keyframe in the group)
Back one frame	Left Arrow or Page Up	Left Arrow or Page Up
Forward one frame	Right Arrow or Page Down	Right Arrow or Page Down
Back ten frames	Shift + Left Arrow or Shift + Page Up	Shift + Left Arrow or Shift Page Up
Forward ten frames	Shift + Right Arrow or Shift + Page Down	Shift + Right Arrow or Shift + Page Down

Move to the beginning of the timeline	Home	Home
Move to the end of the timeline	End	End
Move to the beginning of the work area	Shift + Home	Shift + Home
Move to the end of the work area	Shift + End	Shift + End
Move to In point of the current layer	Up Arrow	Up Arrow
Move to the Out point of the current layer	Down Arrow	Down Arrow
Back 1 second	Shift + Up Arrow	Shift + Up Arrow
Foward 1 second	Shift + Down Arrow	Shift + Down Arrow
Return a rotated document to its original orientation	Esc	Esc

Keys for the Brush Panel.

Result	Windows Shortcut	Mac OS Shortcut

Delete brush	Alt-click brush	Option-click brush
Rename brush	Double-click brush	Double-click brush
Change brush size	Alt + right-click + drag left or right	Ctrl + Option + drag left or right
Decrease/increase brush softness/hardness	Alt + right-click + drag up or down	Ctrl + Option + drag up or down
Select previous/next brush size	, (comma) or . (period)	, (comma) or . (period)
Select first/last brush	Shift + , (comma) or . (period)	Shift + , (comma) or . (period)
Display precise cross hair for brushes	Caps Lock or Shift + Caps Lock	Caps Lock
Toggle airbrush option	Shift + Alt + P	Shift + Option + P

Keys for the Channels Panel.

Note:

If you prefer channel shortcuts starting with Ctrl/Command + 1 for red, choose Edit > Keyboard Shortcuts, and select Use Legacy Channel Shortcuts.

Result	Windows Shortcut	Mac OS Shortcut
Select individual channels	Ctrl + 3 (red), 4 (green), 5 (blue)	Command + 3 (red), 4 (green), 5 (blue)
Select composite channel	Ctrl + 2	Command + 2
Load channel as selection	Control-click channel thumbnail, or Alt + Ctrl + 3 (red), 4 (green), 5 (blue)	Command-click channel thumbnail, or Option + Command + 3 (red), 4 (green), 5 (blue)
Add to current selection	Control + Shift-click channel thumbnail	Command + Shift-click channel thumbnail
Subtract from current selection	Control + Alt-click channel thumbnail	Command + Option-click channel thumbnail
Intersect with current selection	Control + Shift + Alt-click channel thumbnail	Command + Shift + Option-click channel thumbnail
Set options for Save Selection As Channel button	Alt-click Save Selection As Channel button	Option-click Save Selection As Channel button

Create a new spot channel	Control-click Create New Channel button	Command-click Create New Channel button
Select/deselect multiple color-channel selection	Shift-click color channel	Shift-click color channel
Select/deselect alpha channel and show/hide as a rubylith overlay	Shift-click alpha channel	Shift-click alpha channel
Display channel options	Double-click alpha or spot channel thumbnail	Double-click alpha or spot channel thumbnail
Toggle composite and grayscale mask in Quick Mask mode	~ (tilde)	~ (tilde)

Keys for the Clone Source Panel.

Result	Windows Shortcut	Mac OS Shortcut
Show Clone Source (overlays image)	Alt + Shift	Option + Shift
Nudge Clone Source	Alt + Shift + arrow keys	Option + Shift + arrow keys
Rotate Clone Source	Alt + Shift + < or >	Option + Shift + < or >

Scale (increase or reduce size) Clone Source	Alt + Shift + [or]	Option + Shift + [or]

Keys for the Color Panel.

Result	Windows Shortcut	Mac OS Shortcut
Select background color	Alt-click color in color bar	Option-click color in color bar
Display Color Bar menu	Right-click color bar	Control-click color bar
Cycle through color choices	Shift-click color bar	Shift-click color bar

Keys for the History Panel.

Result	Windows Shortcut	Mac OS Shortcut
Create a new snapshot	Alt + New Snapshot	Option + New Snapshot
Rename snapshot	Double-click snapshot name	Double-click snapshot name
Step forward through image states	Control + Shift + Z	Command + Shift + Z

Step backward through image states	Control + Alt + Z	Command + Option + Z
Duplicate any image state, except the current state	Alt-click the image state	Option-click the image state
Permanently clear history (no Undo)	Alt + Clear History (in History panel pop-up menu)	Option + Clear History (in History panel pop-up menu)

Keys for the Info Panel

Result	Windows Shortcut	Mac OS Shortcut
Change color readout modes	Click eyedropper icon	Click eyedropper icon
Change measurement units	Click crosshair icon	Click crosshair icon

Keys for the Layers Panel.

Result	Windows Shortcut	Mac OS Shortcut
Load layer transparency as a selection	Control-click layer thumbnail	Command-click layer thumbnail

Add to current selection	Control + Shift-click layer thumbnail	Command + Shift-click layer thumbnail
Subtract from current selection	Control + Alt-click layer thumbnail	Command + Option-click layer thumbnail
Intersect with current selection	Control + Shift + Alt-click layer thumbnail	Command + Shift + Option-click layer thumbnail
Load filter mask as a selection	Control-click filter mask thumbnail	Command-click filter mask thumbnail
Group layers	Control + G	Command + G
Ungroup layers	Control + Shift + G	Command + Shift + G
Create/release clipping mask	Control + Alt + G	Command + Option + G
Select all layers	Control + Alt + A	Command + Option + A
Merge visible layers	Control + Shift + E	Command + Shift + E
Create new empty layer with dialog box	Alt-click New Layer button	Option-click New Layer button
Create new layer below target layer	Control-click New Layer button	Command-click New Layer button

Select top layer	Alt + . (period)	Option + . (period)
Select bottom layer	Alt + , (comma)	Option + , (comma)
Add to layer selection in Layers panel	Shift + Alt + [or]	Shift + Option + [or]
Select next layer down/up	Alt + [or]	Option + [or]
Move target layer down/up	Control + [or]	Command + [or]
Merge a copy of all visible layers into target layer	Control + Shift + Alt + E	Command + Shift + Option + E
Merge layers	Highlight layers you want to merge, then Control + E	Highlight the layers you want to merge, then Command + E
Move layer to bottom or top	Control + Shift + [or]	Command + Shift + [or]
Copy current layer to layer below	Alt + Merge Down command from the Panel pop-up menu	Option + Merge Down command from the Panel pop-up menu
Merge all visible layers to a new layer above the currently selected layer	Alt + Merge Visible command from the Panel pop-up menu	Option + Merge Visible command from the Panel pop-up menu

Show/hide this layer/layer group only or all layers/layer groups	Right-click the eye icon	Control-click the eye icon
Show/hide all other currently visible layers	Alt-click the eye icon	Option-click the eye icon
Toggle lock transparency for target layer, or last applied lock	/ (forward slash)	/ (forward slash)
Edit layer effect/style, options	Double-click layer effect/style	Double-click layer effect/style
Hide layer effect/style	Alt-double-click layer effect/style	Option-double-click layer effect/style
Edit layer style	Double-click layer	Double-click layer
Disable/enable vector mask	Shift-click vector mask thumbnail	Shift-click vector mask thumbnail
Open Layer Mask Display Options dialog box	Double-click layer mask thumbnail	Double-click layer mask thumbnail
Toggle layer mask on/off	Shift-click layer mask thumbnail	Shift-click layer mask thumbnail

Toggle filter mask on/off	Shift-click filter mask thumbnail	Shift-click filter mask thumbnail
Toggle between layer mask/composite image	Alt-click layer mask thumbnail	Option-click layer mask thumbnail
Toggle between filter mask/composite image	Alt-click filter mask thumbnail	Option-click filter mask thumbnail
Toggle rubylith mode for layer mask on/off	\ (backslash), or Shift + Alt-click	\ (backslash), or Shift + Option-click
Select all type; temporarily select Type tool	Double-click type layer thumbnail	Double-click type layer thumbnail
Create a clipping mask	Alt-click the line dividing two layers	Option-click the line dividing two layers
Rename layer	Double-click the layer name	Double-click the layer name
Edit filter settings	Double-click the filter effect	Double-click the filter effect
Edit the Filter Blending options	Double-click the Filter Blending icon	Double-click the Filter Blending icon
Create new layer group below	Control-click New Group button	Command-click New Group button

current layer/layer set		
Create new layer group with dialog box	Alt-click New Group button	Option-click New Group button
Create layer mask that hides all/selection	Alt-click Add Layer Mask button	Option-click Add Layer Mask button
Create vector mask that reveals all/path area	Control-click Add Layer Mask button	Command-click Add Layer Mask button
Create vector mask that hides all or displays path area	Control + Alt-click Add Layer Mask button	Command + Option-click Add Layer Mask button
Display layer group properties	Right-click layer group and choose Group Properties, or double-click group	Control-click the layer group and choose Group Properties, or double-click group
Select/deselect multiple contiguous layers	Shift-click	Shift-click
Select/deselect multiple discontiguous layers	Control-click	Command-click

Note:

If Kotoeri is your Japanese language input method, the "Toggle rubylith mode for layer mask on/off" shortcut starts an action in Kotoeri. Please switch to another mode (for example, "U.S.") to enable this shortcut.

Keys for the Layer Comps Panel.

Result	Windows Shortcut	Mac OS Shortcut
Create new layer comp without the New Layer Comp box	Alt-click Create New Layer Comp button	Option-click Create New Layer Comp button
Open Layer Comp Options dialog box	Double-click layer comp	Double-click layer comp
Rename in-line	Double-click layer comp name	Double-click layer comp name
Select/deselect multiple contiguous layer comps	Shift-click	Shift-click
Select/deselect multiple discontiguous layer comps	Control-click	Command-click

Keys for the Paths Panel

Result	Windows Shortcut	Mac OS Shortcut
Load path as selection	Control-click pathname	Command-click pathname
Add path to selection	Control + Shift-click pathname	Command + Shift-click pathname
Subtract path from selection	Control + Alt-click pathname	Command + Option-click pathname
Retain intersection of path as selection	Control + Shift + Alt-click pathname	Command + Shift + Option-click pathname
Hide path	Control + Shift + H	Command + Shift + H
Set options for Fill Path with Foreground Color button, Stroke Path with Brush button, Load Path as a Selection button, Make Work Path from Selection button, and Create New Path button	Alt-click button	Option-click button

Keys for the Swatches Panel.

Result	Windows Shortcut	Mac OS Shortcut
Create new swatch from foreground color	Click in empty area of panel	Click in empty area of panel
Set swatch color as background color	Control-click swatch	Command-click swatch
Delete swatch	Alt-click swatch	Option-click swatch

Keys for 3D tools (Photoshop Extended).

Result	Windows Shortcut	Mac OS Shortcut
Enable 3D object tools	K	K
Enable 3D camera tools	N	N
Hide nearest surface	Alt + Ctrl + X	Option + Command + X
Show all surfaces	Alt + Shift + Ctrl + X	Option + Shift + Command + X

3D Object Tool	Right-click (Windows) / Control-click (Mac OS)	Alt (Windows) / Option (Mac OS)
Rotate	Changes to Drag tool	Changes to Roll tool
Roll	Changes to Slide tool	Changes to Rotate tool
Drag	Changes to Orbit tool	Changes to Slide tool
Slide	Changes to Roll tool	Changes to Drag tool
Scale	Scales on the Z plane	Scales on the Z plane

Note:

To scale on the Y plane, hold down the Shift key.

Camera Tool	Right-click (Windows) / Control-click (Mac OS)	Alt (Windows) / Option (Mac OS)
Orbit	Changes to Drag tool	Changes to Roll tool
Roll	Changes to Slide tool	Changes to Rotate tool
Pan	Changes to Orbit tool	Changes to Slide tool
Walk	Changes to Roll tool	Changes to Drag tool

Keys for Measurement (Photoshop Extended).

Result	Windows Shortcut	Mac OS Shortcut
Record a measurement	Shift + Control + M	Shift + Command + M
Deselects all measurements	Control + D	Command + D
Selects all measurements	Control + A	Command + A
Hide/show all measurements	Shift + Control + H	Shift + Command + H
Removes a measurement	Backspace	Delete
Nudge the measurement	Arrow keys	Arrow keys
Nudge the measurement in increments	Shift + arrow keys	Shift + arrow keys
Extend/shorten selected measurement	Ctrl + Left/Right Arrow key	Command + Left/Right Arrow key
Extend/shorten selected measurement in increments	Shift + Ctrl + Left/Right Arrow key	Shift + Command + Left/Right Arrow key

Rotate selected measurement	Ctrl + Up/Down Arrow key	Command + Up/Down Arrow key
Rotate selected measurement in increments	Shift + Ctrl + Up/Down Arrow key	Shift + Command + Up/Down Arrow key

Keys for DICOM files (Photoshop Extended).

Result	Windows Shortcut	Mac OS Shortcut
Zoom tool	Z	Z
Hand tool	H	H
Window Level tool	W	W
Select all frames	Control + A	Command + A
Deselect all frames except the current frame	Control + D	Command + D
Navigate through frames	Arrow keys	Arrow keys

Keys for Extract and Pattern Maker (optional plug-ins).

Result (Extract and	Windows Shortcut	Mac OS Shortcut

Pattern Maker)		
Fit in window	Control + 0	Command + 0
Zoom in	Control + + (plus)	Command + + (plus)
Zoom out	Control + - (hyphen)	Command + - (hyphen)
Cycle through controls on right from top	Tab	Tab
Cycle through controls on right from bottom	Shift + Tab	Shift + Tab
Temporarily activate Hand tool	Spacebar	Spacebar
Change Cancel to Reset	Alt	Option
Result (Extract only)	**Windows Shortcut**	**Mac OS Shortcut**
Edge Highlighter tool	B	B
Fill tool	G	G
Eyedropper tool	I	I
Cleanup tool	C	C
Edge Touchup tool	T	T
Toggle between Edge	Alt + Edge Highlighter/Eraser tool	Option + Edge Highlighter/Eraser tool

Highlighter tool and Eraser tool		
Toggle Smart Highlighting	Control with Edge Highlighter tool selected	Command with Edge Highlighter tool selected
Remove current highlight	Alt + Delete	Option + Delete
Highlight entire image	Control + Delete	Command + Delete
Fill foreground area and preview extraction	Shift-click with Fill tool selected	Shift-click with Fill tool selected
Move mask when Edge Touchup tool is selected	Control-drag	Command-drag
Add opacity when Cleanup tool is selected	Alt-drag	Option-drag
Toggle Show menu options in preview between Original and Extracted	X	X
Enable Cleanup and Edge Touchup tools before preview	Shift + X	Shift + X

Cycle through Display menu in preview from top to bottom	F	F
Cycle through Display menu in preview from bottom to top	Shift + F	Shift + F
Decrease/increase brush size by 1	Down Arrow/Up Arrow in Brush Size text box[†]	Down Arrow or Up Arrow in Brush Size text box[†]
Decrease/increase brush size by 1	Left Arrow/Right Arrow with Brush Size Slider showing[†]	Left Arrow/Right Arrow with Brush Size Slider showing[†]
Set strength of Cleanup or Edge Touch-up tool	0–9	0–9
[†]Hold down Shift to decrease/increase by 10		
Result (Pattern Maker only)	**Windows Shortcut**	**Mac OS Shortcut**
Delete current selection	Control + D	Command + D
Undo a selection move	Control + Z	Command + Z
Generate or generate again	Control + G	Command + G

Intersect with current selection	Shift + Alt + select	Shift + Option + select
Toggle view: original/genera ted pattern	X	X
Go to first tile in Tile History	Home	Home
Go to last tile in Tile History	End	End
Go to previous tile in Tile History	Left Arrow, Page Up	Left Arrow, Page Up
Go to next tile in Tile History	Right Arrow, Page Down	Right Arrow, Page Down
Delete current tile from Tile History	Delete	Delete
Nudge selection when viewing the original	Right Arrow, Left Arrow, Up Arrow, or Down Arrow	Right Arrow, Left Arrow, Up Arrow, or Down Arrow
Increase selection nudging when viewing the original	Shift + Right Arrow, Left Arrow, Up Arrow, or Down Arrow	Shift + Right Arrow, Left Arrow, Up Arrow, or Down Arrow

Customer's Page.

This page is for customers who enjoyed Adobe Photoshop CC Keyboard Shortcuts for Windows and Macintosh OS.

Our beloved and respectable reader, we thank you very much for your patronage. Please we will appreciate it more if you rate and review this book; that is if it was helpful to you. Thank you.

Download Our EBooks Today For Free.

In order to appreciate our customers, we have made some of our titles available at 0.00. They are totally free. Feel free to get a copy of the free titles.

Here are books we give to our customers free of charge:

(A) For Keyboard Shortcuts in Windows check:

Windows 7 Keyboard Shortcuts.

(B) For Keyboard Shortcuts in Office 2016 for Windows check:

Word 2016 Keyboard Shortcuts For Windows.

(C) For Keyboard Shortcuts in Office 2016 for Mac check:

OneNote 2016 Keyboard Shortcuts For Macintosh.

Follow this link to download any of the titles listed above for free.

Note: Feel free to download them from our website or your favorite bookstore today. Thank you.

Other Books By This Publisher.

Titles for single programs under Shortcut Matters Series are not part of this list.

S/N	Title	Series
Series A: Limits Breaking Quotes.		
1	Discover Your Key Christian Quotes	Limits Breaking Quotes
Series B: Shortcut Matters.		
1	Windows 7 Shortcuts	Shortcut Matters
2	Windows 7 Shortcuts & Tips	Shortcut Matters
3	Windows 8.1 Shortcuts	Shortcut Matters
4	Windows 10 Shortcut Keys	Shortcut Matters
5	Microsoft Office 2007 Keyboard Shortcuts For Windows.	Shortcut Matters

6	Microsoft Office 2010 Shortcuts For Windows.	Shortcut Matters
7	Microsoft Office 2013 Shortcuts For Windows.	Shortcut Matters
8	Microsoft Office 2016 Shortcuts For Windows.	Shortcut Matters
9	Microsoft Office 2016 Keyboard Shortcuts For Macintosh.	Shortcut Matters
10	Top 11 Adobe Programs Keyboard Shortcuts	Shortcut Matters
11	Top 10 Email Service Providers Keyboard Shortcuts	Shortcut Matters
12	Hot Corel Programs Keyboard Shortcuts	Shortcut Matters
13	Top 10 Browsers Keyboard Shortcuts	Shortcut Matters
14	Microsoft Browsers Keyboard Shortcuts.	Shortcut Matters
15	Popular Email Service Providers Keyboard Shortcuts	Shortcut Matters
16	Professional Video Editing with Keyboard Shortcuts.	Shortcut Matters
17	Popular Web Browsers Keyboard Shortcuts.	Shortcut Matters

Series C: Teach Yourself.

| 1 | Teach Yourself Computer Fundamentals | Teach Yourself |
| 2 | Teach Yourself Computer Fundamentals Workbook | Teach Yourself |

Series D: For Painless Publishing

1	Self-Publish it with CreateSpace.	For Painless Publishing
2	Where is my money? Now solved for Kindle and CreateSpace	For Painless Publishing
3	Describe it on Amazon	For Painless Publishing